THE POISON IN
OUR SYSTEM

CARL J. FRIEDRICH

COUNCIL FOR DEMOCRACY
285 MADISON AVENUE • NEW YORK

THE BATTLE FOR THE MIND OF AMERICA

THERE HAS BEEN a Battle of France, and a Battle of Britain, and a Battle of the Atlantic — yet the most important battle of all is the battle of and for the Mind of America. Hitler knows it and has known it right along. According to Hermann Rauschning, Hitler's "voice of destruction" was heard saying: "Artillery preparation before an attack as during the World War will be replaced in the future war by the psychological dislocation of the adversary through revolutionary propaganda." To neglect *this* invasion of America is to act like an ostrich. All the appeasers like to dwell on the imaginary invasion by tanks and troopships; many of them do not realize that in doing so they are doing what Hitler wants them to. Exploiting every discontent, they tell us that Hitler is bound to win, thus spreading defeatism and undermining our morale, our belief in the future of democracy.

But words are not the most important weapon of the propagandist today. Many have spoken of the War of Words. Hitler does his most effective propagandizing through *acts*. A strike in a key plant, initiated through totalitarian agents, whether Stalin's or Hitler's, accomplishes more in one day than a week's outpouring of the printing presses. It depresses morale, it stirs up strife and mutual denunciations; some shout, "Treason, treason!" while others demand that "strikers be electrocuted" or managers jailed and plants taken over by the government. "Psychological dislocation" — this key to Nazi strategy of terror in this country cannot be combated by adopting the methods of the totalitarian despots themselves. A strengthening, not a weakening, of democratic methods is in order. As Edmond Taylor says of French morale at one point in *The Strategy of Terror* (incidentally by far the best analysis of the Nazi technique of morale destruction), "Really democracy in this country [France] has already broken down because all groups approve the repressive use of authority when it operates against their enemies." Here is the core, the decisive front in the battle for the mind of America. Thousands and tens of thousands have been succumbing to totalitarian poison, not only on the appeasers' side, but on the belligerents' side as well. *Time* carried a letter the other day from a woman who demanded that all Germans be sterilized. I am sure she thought herself extremely patriotic. In fact, her mind had become Hitlerized, racial hatred generating senseless physical violence. Without knowing it, she had become the *most dangerous* fifth columnist in our midst: the person who has lost faith in democracy, in civilized methods, in Christianity.

The fifth columnist was first recognized in the Spanish Civil War. He was suddenly discovered stalking behind the back of fighting armies, ready to support the work of the columns at the front. He has grown in stature ever since as the live symbol of our age — an age of world-wide civil war which recognizes no national boundaries. But whereas in Spain it seemed to be a war between Communism and Fascism, or between Stalinism and Hitlerism, it has since turned into a war between totalitarianism and democracy. According to some, it was that even in Spain, with the Stalinists stirring the witches' cauldron, as they seem to be doing so effectively today. Astute observers agree in accusing Moscow of a persistent policy of aggravating disturbances out of a deep-rooted conviction that "capitalist democracy" is doomed. In this, their enmity toward democracy, lies the securest link of Stalinists with Hitlerites and Fascists, and since men work together because they share their hatreds, democracy finds itself today unmistakably confronted with a world-wide coalition of anti-democratic forces. Hence the problem of anti-democratic propaganda, what it is and what it does, is a much broader and deeper issue than is commonly assumed. Yet, our dilemma is even more profound than this double-barreled enmity.

If the democratic tradition were a fanatical "faith" in some particular panacea, we could undertake to suppress its critics as anti-democratic, and if we used enough force we might hope to prevail. Unfortunately, the need for criticism springs from the very core of our constitutional and democratic tradition, as does the positive conviction of the value of diversity and contrast. To put it paradoxically, democratic faith insists upon its own inadequacy. It almost glories in its imperfection. It invites its own change. If we are good democrats, we are agreed upon the value of disagreement. We are agreed to respect the "opinion we hate," to use Justice Holmes's famous phrase. This raises the question today: Are the forces opposed to democracy, the anti-democratic fifth columnists, included in such respect, or are they to be suppressed? If the latter, where does suppression begin?

What Is Propaganda?

There are many who would simply answer this question by a distinction between constructive criticism and lying propaganda. Indeed, everywhere legal discriminations are being attempted that would outlaw Communists, Nazis, and Fascists as enemies of our democracy. That they are enemies of our democracy there can be no doubt. But what if they come back with the retort that their hostility to democracy is merely due to their solicitude for America's future? That democracy is the past, and that America should mount the wave of the future and ride it? What is propaganda anyway? Some have mockingly defined it as "the opinion of the other fellow." Others have condemned it by making it synonymous with intentional misrepresentation of the facts. But who will probe the hearts of men and speak with certainty of a fellow's intentions? How, then, shall we define propaganda?

A recent doctoral dissertation at Harvard listed several dozen definitions of the word. In my research work I have found it helpful to emphasize that carrying on propaganda means "communicating information, true or false, in order to get people to do or to keep them from doing specific things, like joining an organization, making a contribution, or waving a flag." But there can be little doubt that most people do not use the word "propaganda" in such a neutral way. Most men in the street think of lies when they hear of propaganda. By doing so they blind themselves to what are by far the most dangerous onslaughts upon our morale, our confidence in the future of democracy. Though the totalitarian propaganda strategists unquestionably use misrepresentations and lies continually, they know that the most effective propaganda is the propaganda of true facts. They also know that Pilate's question still contains a potent point in that the truth is not exactly self-evident in matters of real importance.

Unfortunately, the most important issues are entirely controversial. Our judgment of what is right is not rooted in facts, but in opinion, in belief, in faith. Take such a question as whether America is really a democracy or, rather, a plutocracy in disguise. Men of good will and ardent democratic faith have disagreed on that question. Yet, does not the answer vitally affect our morale at this time? We may have our own answer, call it a false alternative or whatever you please, but if the Goebbels ministry keeps pouring out the dispatches highlighting this symbol "plutocracy" we soon find ourselves confronted with the question: Shall we look upon everyone who calls America a plutocracy as a potential or actual fifth columnist, or shall we allow Goebbels to undermine democratic morale? And where again shall we draw the line? Is anyone who talks about "classes" in America a suspect carrier of Marxist-Stalinist poison, or is Stalin going to be permitted to break up our social structure into mutually hostile groups?

Reporting The News

The very form of these questions shows that we cannot do either. Discriminating judgment is required in all such instances. If we believe in democracy, we believe in the judgment of the common man. If we can make him understand the methods of totalitarian propaganda, we shall impregnate him against its temptations. Unfortunately at the present time not even the editors of most newspapers and magazines in the United States understand these methods. This, curiously enough, is due not to their complexity, but to their extreme simplicity. By worrying about the fifth columnist under our bed, we overlook the fifth columnist right in front of us — staring us in the face as we look at the latest news of our morning paper. The most potent Nazi propaganda is carried by our best magazines. To offer one illustration:—

The magazine *Life,* with millions of readers in this country, published a few weeks ago a short autobiographical piece presumably written by a German bomber. Innocently it was suggested that the thing was authentic, but that the name of the author could not, in accordance with the rules of the German censor, be revealed. I may be entirely wrong, but the piece when analyzed seemed to me clearly a synthetic product of the Goebbels ministry of propaganda. No doubt the editors of *Life* did not see it that way. But, if space permitted, it would be easy to show this point by point. Go back to that article and do it yourself. Ask yourself, as you read these sentences, What was this phrase to accomplish, what reaction was that to bring about? You will find that the piece was to get across the following ideas, among others: "These fliers are tremendously efficient, these fliers are human and regret the destruction they bring; German soldiers are Nazis, Austrians are Germans; these fliers, these Germans, these Nazis, are an overpowering wave — there is no use in resisting them," and so forth. The thing is a perfect piece of ammunition in the battle of the mind. Though couched in words, it is presented as a fact, an act, a revelation. It is unwise to assume that any Nazi flier today would be permitted to write such a piece by himself, even if the representative of the American magazine offering to publish it had been his lifelong friend. He would have to report the overture; the skillful manipulators in the Goebbels ministry would do the rest. In doing it these clever strategists would build up their extensive knowledge of the American public. They would do it, confident that the American reader would not make a careful study to discover the synthetic elements. How many *Life* readers made such an analysis, do you think? None that I talked to ever did. They were depressed; they felt that the position of England was hopeless. "You can't fight them," they said.

The very same thing is happening day in and day out when we read the papers. The editor believes he is doing his duty if he publishes side by side the two dispatches, one from Berlin, the other from London. In so doing, he places a tremendous responsibility upon the reader. Not merely the task of telling himself that he is reading propaganda; the British, too, make propaganda. But to read a Berlin dispatch or a Moscow dispatch without bad after effects one has to understand and keep in mind how this black magic works. Remember, in the first place, that the propagandists in Berlin do not have to worry about a hostile opposition, quick to criticize every mistake made; they can, for example, lie about the people they control without having to fear an exposé that boomerangs. From this standpoint, our correspondents in places like Berlin are not "correspondents" in the old sense.

If you want to get a picture of the limitations under which they work, read Whitaker's recent reports *after* he got out.

What is even more important: the totalitarians' objective is to discredit democracy — simply because they know that the greatest depressive of morale is being in doubt about the eventual victory. In short, these ministries of propaganda are plotting continually, not merely to misinform us, but to set in motion psychic disturbances which will make us defeatist. "Democracy is dead," "Britain is lost" — these are the inferences they wish to insinuate by the news items they release. The wire services — AP, UP, and the rest — are in a key position. They naturally pride themselves on the *speed* with which they handle their dispatches. Recently it was said that "the average time lapse between the arrival of a bulletin from abroad at the cable desk (of the AP) and its receipt by the newspapers is less than a minute." This is a brilliant technical achievement. Yet one might wish that there were a little more thought given to the symbols embedded in the items from anti-democratic headquarters to make sure that they are a necessary part of the news. Why should American newspapers, for example, repeat over and over again the Berlin-manufactured symbol "annihilated"? According to such news items, the British forces were thus "annihilated" at least half a dozen times. Each time the word was used a psychic disturbance of far-reaching consequence was set in train in millions of American minds. It's a terrible thing, this symbolic invasion from Mars. Is it fair to expect the average American newspaper reader to cope with it? One might wonder whether there could not be a series of "schools", informational meetings where editors and copy writers all over the land might learn from men like Edmond Taylor, Otto Tolischus or William Shirer how Dr. Goebbels conducts his business. There are such meetings for safety officers every month now in most states of the Union in order to acquaint them with the technique of the Fifth Column. The Column of the Anti-Democratic Symbols is the most dangerous!

After all, why not utilize the insight of observers who have been watching this game until they are nearly ready to despair? There is, for example, Matthew Gordon, specialist in CBS's New York office on foreign news. For such observers who have caught on, reading the newspapers is like watching your friend at a chess game, tongue-tied, watching him being ensnared — while you know that the stakes are life and liberty and the pursuit of happiness.

As long as "news" is being handed to us direct from Nazi headquarters in the words which Dr. Goebbels has carefully chosen to produce the maximum adverse effect upon our general psychic well-being, we will have to defend ourselves as best we can. Commentators, such as Raymond Gram Swing, help to produce a measure of detachment. But we must do a lot of work ourselves. It's like insisting upon patronizing a restaurant some of whose food is known to be poison. We must realize that a psychological offensive is being waged *against us* in these very dispatches. As one observant editor put it to me: "I know that in my case I begin my reading of the Berlin report with the reservation that the Nazis characteristically use misleading figures and that their whole intent and purpose is to hornswoggle my mind. But the fact remains that I do read what they intend me to read, and that even though I remain vigilant, some of the poison does remain in my system." The man, an unusually able citizen, is right of course. The poison distilled by Dr. Goebbels is entering our system, because we are watching for the wrong danger. We are not doing enough when we worry about the "misleading figures", about the confusion of the mind. For the aim of the Nazis is to get us into an emotional stew. Their method is to manipulate the symbols. This poison is much harder to resist and to fight. Here is typical illustration.

"Dunkirking" The News

As soon as the British began to fight side by side with the Greeks, the Nazis commenced to predict another Dunkirk. This symbol (which practically all American news dispatches accepted as part of the news) was built up into a key position, because it magnified the (probable) British withdrawal into a major catastrophe. Hence, when it occurred, it depressed us much more than it need have done. Quite a few of our commentators played right into their hands, unfortunately, by beginning to talk about the battle of the Mediterranean, the most decisive phase of the war and all that. From the Nazi viewpoint, this build-up, had, of course, many other advantages: from here the interpretation travelled to Australia, to Canada and to Britain, causing a major morale upset. It also had its influence right in the Balkans.

Another symbol the Nazis played up with increasing volume during the Balkan struggle was that of "perfidious Albion." The claim was advanced, even before the fight got under way, that the British were withdrawing their troops. From Berlin it was pretended that only the most determined efforts on the part of the German army produced contact with the British forces. Though primarily destined for Greek consumption, this notion of the British perfidy in drawing other people into the war to pull the chestnuts out of the fire for them fits in quite neatly with the symbolism of appeasement in this country. "Let those who started the war, finish it . . . " is the echo of the Goebbels's line. Readers and editors take all such items as if they were just ordinary everyday news. But in point of fact all these seemingly disconnected stories fall into definite patterns, worked out by scientifically trained specialists who know how the American press works, how to arrange a build-up, how to "make news." What is more, these practitioners of the art of psychic massage know how their poison works, they understand the black magic of terror. Such news isn't news in the old-fashioned way; it is directed news—but directed toward what? Toward the destruction of our morale, our self-confidence, our readiness to act in the defense of American democracy. Feinting, intimidation, suspense . . . the witch doctors in Berlin know that we cordially detest them and all they stand for. But that does not discourage them. It has been true of all their other enemies, most of all their German enemies.

Nazi Technique

In short, the greatest difficulty in dealing with Nazi propaganda arises from the fact that Nazi methods are not understood. Many people assume that the totalitarians rely upon highly secretive procedures. Their fear and anxiety combine with lurid journalism to create a fog of emotional agitation which is precisely what the Nazis are seeking to produce. Hitler's declared purpose of "psychological dislocation" finds its strongest ally in our own weaknesses. The surprising successes that Goebbels's methods have scored are in part due to the fact the they are built upon cynical insight into human frailities.

One of those simple insights into how the human mind works is this: only the more thoughtful examine major premises. When a doubtful assertion is being made, most of us plunge into an argument over it without further ado. From this simple and incontrovertible fact the Nazis have derived a most effective method; when they want to get something across to us, whom they know to be suspicious of their assertions, they do not assert it, but assume it in a challenging proposition. As a result, the major premise will be accepted by friends and enemies of their explicit assertion. Here is how it works. The Nazis desired that we in America should believe that the Nazis are going to win the war. If they had simply asserted it, the other side would have denied the assertion. Doubt, at least, would remain strong. So, instead, they proceeded through various emissaries (including French pro-Vichy "sources") to plant the idea that "after the war America should trade with a victorious Germany." Whether we like Hitler or not, we must deal with him, ran the legend. "If the Nazis win, let's not be sentimental — business is business. It is all an imperialist war anyway."

Today these formulas are familiar. Reputable men have sponsored them; others have combated them. But most of those who have taken a stand against such views have walked into the Nazis' trap. They have said; "No, we must not deal with a victorious Hitler" — thereby swelling the chorus of voices holding that Hitler might be victorious. Many publicists have gone great lengths in depicting what the world will be like after a Nazi victory, thereby feeding the Nazis' essential premise: "A Nazi victory, if not a certainty, is at any rate a strong possibility." Insight into Nazi propaganda strategy would have made these publicists, writers, and columnists pause to ask the vital question: "Who said that the Nazis are winning the war?" Such questioning of the major premise would have spoiled the Nazi game.

Many similar examples can be given to show how this principle has been employed by the Nazis in the past. Their entire appeasement propaganda in France and England was built on such propositions. The assertion itself might be couched in a question: " Should the Sudeten Germans be incorporated by negotiation or by occupation?" (Major premise: "They will be incorporated.") "Should the United States aid Britain, or shouldn't she?" (Major premise: "No interest of the United States herself is involved in the war.") In these and many similar instances the Nazis succeeded in getting their foes as well as their friends to popularize the points which they wished to get across. As to the present drive to get us to accept a Hitler-dominated world, it is revealing to note the typical crescendo in the premises: (1) *if* Hitler wins, (2) *when* Hitler wins, (3) *since* Hitler is winning, (4) *because* Hitler is winning . . . The Nazis have made such headway with their most recent campaign that if a man gets up and speaks on "After Hitler — What?" as I have done recently he's looked upon with some amazement. Many have already come to believe that Hitler will win this war. So if someone gets up and says, "I believe Hitler will be defeated," people feel cheered by such a firm belief. Facts speak louder than words, and no one knows it better than Hitler. Hence the propaganda of the act, of which I have already spoken.

PROPAGANDA OF THE ACT

How did the propaganda of the act work to support the Nazis' contention that they were to win the war? They used a variety of devices. Last summer German firms throughout Latin America took orders for fall delivery. They even posted cash bonds to guarantee performance of the contract. They are reported to be doing it again right now. It was very amusing when information about those contracts first "leaked through" — a New York business man whispered it into my ear as "inside dope." He was incredulous when I suggested it might be a propaganda trick. There can be little doubt that this propaganda was destined for just such business men. Would they not ask themselves the anxious question, "What will become of my war orders for Britain?"

The Nazis used another device for influencing German workingmen in this country, particularly men in key defense jobs. Such a man one day received a letter from some business concern which read as follows: "Dear Sir: As soon as Germany has won this war, German workers will have undreamt-of opportunities for lucrative employment in the Greater *Reich*. You as a skilled mechanic will no doubt be desirous of participating in such opportunities, particularly as the pro-British factions in this country may deprive you of your job here. Since the openings will be filled in order of application, we suggest that you communicate with us at once, so that you may get on the list and thereby not lose this golden opportunity . . . " I have seen these letters and examined their authenticity. No matter what the worker does with them, they leave him affected. Propaganda of the act!

Strikes

Strikes are, of course, rooted in maladjustments between management and labor.   But it is asserted by persons who have made careful surveys that Communist leaders and Nazi agents have often been active behind the scenes.   Mr. H. W. Barclay, editor of *Mill and Factory*, who has spent several months investigating the background of strikes in defense plants, has secured extensive testimony from workers to that effect.

No matter how difficult it may be to evaluate the data gathered by investigators such as Mr. Barclay (and there is plenty of evidence, one hears, in the Department of Justice and other official agencies to support his findings), such evidence for Nazi complicity in aggravating our difficulties seems credible for the simple reason that these strikes fit so completely into the plans of Berlin.   As I suggested earlier, they provide perfect material for "propaganda of the act."   Should we then outlaw them?   Not at all; for such outlawry would simply provide another "act" to demonstrate the failure of democracy.

Indeed, if there were not material discontents, manifest failures of our democracy, no agent could bring on strikes.   But can we hope at this moment to right all wrongs, and solve all the problems of our all-too-human democracy?   The counsel of perfection is a potent weapon of the cynic.   Nihilism — that is, destructive criticism, scoffing disbelief in everything and in anything — feeds upon an insistence that there should not be any flaws in a building, else it must come down.   What is our most potent defense against such enemies of the republic?   Some want to suppress them; to organize spy hunts, jail every Communist, shoot every Bundsman.   Are such proceedings going to strengthen our faith in the future of democracy?   If we cannot resist the lure of force, if we allow ourselves to fall prey to the temptation of violence, we are weakening our own position. Shall we look on, then, with indifference? Most assuredly not. There are important things that we can do, that we must do.

Organizations

Out in Kansas City the Reverend L. M. Birkhead, head of the Friends of Democracy, has been waging practically a one-man battle against the infiltration of such material. His story is an interesting one.

As a minister out in Kansas, he became aware, soon after the Nazis came into power, that there were curious currents of un-American undemocratic ideas becoming aggressively vocal. He noticed their resemblance to Nazi formulas. So, in typical American fashion, he went across to Germany to see what it was all about. He has a dramatic story to tell about his explorations, which finally landed him in propaganda headquarters. Herr Vogt had just succeeded Putzi Hanfstaengl. With the naiveté of the zealot, Herr Vogt ended up by showing Birkhead all his correspondence with Winrod, Edmondson, Colonel Sanctuary, and the rest of the native American anti-democratic front.

So when Birkhead came back to the United States in the fall of 1935 he began to investigate, combat, and publicize these poisoners of our mind. There were many names here that nobody in America ever heard of—and quite a few have since been forgotten. Any one who desired detailed information can find plenty of material in such books as William S. Schlamm's *The Second War of Independence*. There is, of course, an amazing array of organizations of this type. Even today the atmosphere of conspiracy which the Nazi spread around lends itself to cheap political racketeering. For many of these organizations are still very much alive. Writes Schlamm: "The totalitarian invasion's shock troops are deeply entrenched in America's soil. While the United States has only begun to arm against a future military aggression, the real, the modern war of decomposition has been going on for years." Many of these organizations do not admit promoting Nazism or Fascism in the United States. Of course not. But their publications reveal them as poisoned by Nazi-Fascist thinking. Not only do their publications reveal their Nazi-Fascist thinking, but investigation of the personnel carrying on the work of these organizations proves it. The proselytizing of National Socialism is usually promoted behind the convenient facade of patriotic American names. They illustrate the quip that "when Fascism comes to America it will come in the garb of Americanism."

Dr. Birkhead was instrumental in defeating Winrod when the latter sought nomination on the Republican ticket for Congress. He played a similar role in stopping the Coughlin build-up that was engulfing the United States last year. Later, through his New York office, he helped in blocking the McWilliams drive for Congress.

His technique is an interesting combination of research, public information, and political campaigning. In the Kansas campaign, for example, he first gathered all the material, then published it in pamphlet form. This pamphlet, entitled "Winrod of Wichita, Arch-Apologist of Hitler," was then sent to every precinct captain in the Congressional district. Backed by an endorsement from William Allen White and Alfred Landon, the pamphlet punctured the Winrod bubble. The material on Coughlin was furnished to 15,000 leading Catholics. Dr. Birkhead rightly stressed the importance of getting the information to the key people rather than merely "getting it out." The Friends of Democracy have recently released some striking material which they collected on the activities of the America First Committee.

This method of counteracting anti-democratic and subversive activities is much more effective than bottling it up.

Domestic Foreign Language Broadcasts

It has been suggested that foreign-language radio and press should be outlawed. Here, it is felt we have the channel, mysterious, inaccessible, through which the totalitarians commune with the American people. It is a proven fact that foreign-language broadcasts were extensively used by totalitarian propagandists. In a number of Eastern seaboard stations practically all the news announcers and commentators were known to be Fascist sympathizers, if not actual members of the Fascist Party. I do not wish to mention them by symbol, because their practices have since been discontinued. Not only was there daily open extolling of Mussolini and his works, but frank denunciation of democracy and America. Programs equally blatant in their subversive intent were heard on some of the German-language broadcast stations in the Middle West (German-language broadcasts are less numerous than Italian, Yiddish, Polish, and Spanish). When anti-Fascist, pro-democratic persons wanted to get a hearing on these stations, they were almost always given the cold shoulder.

Counteractions

When these conditions were first brought to the attention of a broader public, many people wanted to outlaw foreign-language broadcasts altogether. That was a year or so ago. Wisely, the Federal Communications Commission, under James Fly, counseled moderation. "Let us find out the facts," they said. A questionnaire was sent to all stations broadcasting in foreign tongues, asking for very detailed information as to content, sponsorship, and the rest. The National Association of Broadcasters set up a Committee to study the situation and make recommendations. The Office of Radio Research at Columbia and the Radiobroadcasting Research Project at Harvard undertook to study the listeners' reactions and to ascertain how and by whom these programs were controlled. All these inquiries revealed that the propagandists who had so comfortably installed themselves in this forgotten corner were beating a hasty retreat as soon as the spotlight of publicity was turned on them. They also showed that such foreign-language broadcasts reach a group of non-readers, hundreds of thousands of foreign-born Americans who cannot be effectively reached by other channels of communication. What is needed and wanted is an effective use of such broadcasts for pro-democracy work. Thus the Mazzini Society has recently shaped such a program, which has been offered over WHOM in New York. Recordings have been made available to other stations. The Department of Justice is at present engaged in making its striking series of broadcasts, "I'm an American," available in Italian and German. Many outstanding persons of unquestioned loyalty to democracy and its ideals have participated in the series.

Much more of this sort of thing needs to be done. American firms with business interest among foreign-language groups — the great mass-consumption advertisers of soap, gas, breakfast foods, and so forth — should make it their business to give really thoughtful attention to the possibilities of utilizing their promotional work along this line. Some striking beginnings have been made in the field of soap operas. Because the stations carrying foreign-language broadcasts are usually small, they have to watch their pennies and find it difficult to devote much time to sustainining programs of purely public interest. If, at the same time, the Department of Justice's Nationality Unit and the Federal Communications Commission's Monitoring Service continue on the alert, our concern over foreign-language broadcasts of domestic origin need not cause us to demand their discontinuance.

There has, however, cropped up a new device which may not be so easily dealt with. An outfit which calls itself The Almanac Music Company, Inc., has recently brought out a series of phonograph records, called "Songs for John Doe." These recordings are distributed under the innocuous appeal: "Sing out for Peace." Yet they are strictly subversive and illegal. Sung to such familiar tunes as "Billy Boy," they ridicule the American defense effort, democracy, and the army. Whether Nazi or Communist financed, their general spirit is well indicated by the following sample:—

C for Conscription

It's C for Conscription, and C for Capitol Hill;
C for Conscription and C for Capitol Hill;
It's C for the Congress that passed that goddamned bill.

Another song is called "Plow Under"; it's the first one, and so I guess they like it best. The first verse runs:—

Remember when the AAA
Killed a million hogs a day?
Instead of hogs, it's men today—
Plow the fourth one under!
Plow under, plow under,
Plow under every fourth American boy!

And the last one:—

Now the politicians rant,
"A boy's no better than a cotton plant";
But we are here to say you can't
Plow the fourth one under!

The three records sell for one dollar and you are asked to "play them in your home, play them in your union hall, take them back to your people." Probably some of these songs fall under the criminal provisions of the Selective Service Act, and to that extent it is a matter for the Attorney-General.

But you never can handle situations of this kind democratically by mere suppression. Unless civic groups and individuals will make a determined effort to counteract such appeals by equally effective methods, democratic morale will decline. A variety of organizations has been doing a splendid job here. Station WHA out in Wisconsin has been presenting a dramatic pro-democracy serial on civil liberties showing the deeper issues in the fight for freedom in superb fashion. But perhaps the most remarkable achievement in this field has been the series of radio dramas which The Free Company, under the able chairmanship of James Boyd, has been presenting. Besides Boyd, Saroyan, Sherwood, Benét, Welles, Connelly, MacLeish, Maxwell and Sherwood Anderson, Paul Green, and Walter V. Clark have been some of the writers associated with the series. They are marvels of genuine pro-democracy poetry, broadly gauged in their conception of freedom, and hence suitable for reproduction in every home and schoolroom in the land.

DIRECT FROM EUROPE

FOREIGN BROADCASTS — a continuous stream of "news" and comment has been flowing into this country via short wave from Berlin, Vichy, and Rome, but more particularly from Berlin. This material is, of course, carefully prepared by the clever strategists in the totalitarian war-upon-democracy centres. Listening posts set up in the studios of NBC and CBS, as well as at Princeton University, have accumulated a mass of detailed information on the words and symbols employed to reach the American mind. There can be little question that both sides have continuously utilized this channel for every kind of propaganda. However, from our viewpoint, the all-important difference is that totalitarian propaganda has been anti-democratic. It has sought to undermine our confidence in the future of the institutions under which we live. It has sneered at our defense effort; it has brazenly thrown our pacifism in our face when we found ourselves obliged to adopt the draft to cope with a potential Nazi threat.

How widely are these "poison packages" accepted? Attempts to determine the extent of listening through our national opinion polls, the Gallup poll and the *Fortune* poll, have produced entirely inconclusive results. Interviewers ran into difficulties in getting people to admit that they were listening to such broadcasts. Naturally. Nor is it practicable to gauge the extent of such propaganda by the *number* of listeners. Through such broadcasts the Nazis suggest the *key symbols* which are then carried about throughout the land by their friends, their stooges, and even their enemies. "America is a pluto-democracy" is a typical symbol. "Roosevelt means Rosenfeld" is one of the more vicious anti-Semitic symbols.

Other such word symbols are "America for Americans, Europe for Europeans." "This is Europe's war," "The Jewish-controlled press," "Germany is fighting for the removal of an injustice," "It is good business to be on good terms with the winner," and so forth. It would take us far afield to analyze the particular methods employed by the Nazis during their propaganda campaign to keep America out of the war, to weaken her internal unity, to slow down defense. It is important to keep in mind that this campaign is also designed to maintain the morale of Nazi supporters in this country. Surrounded as they are by a hostile American public, and depressed as they must be by our rapidly rising defense effort, the Nazi short waves reassure them day in and day out that Hitler is going to win in the end — and add to that the wild idea that "America is ours."

Obviously this type of broadcast requires entirely different handling on our part. Since we cannot get at the source and hence cannot prevent its entering the country, so long as we are formally at peace, a continuous and vigorous effort to counteract the effect of these communications is essential. What is even more important is a comprehensive and large-scale attack upon Nazi confidence in the future.

Foreign Mail Restrictions

A little while back the Council For Democracy undertook a rather ingenious bit along these lines. Many people had been annoyed for some time by the extent to which Nazi printed propaganda was flooding this country at the expense of the American post office. All the Nazis had to do was to print it and stamp it; the rest was up to Uncle Sam and the countries between here and Berlin. Yet, all suggestions to stop this paper invasion of the United States by refusal to ship subversive material met with the reasonable, democratic reply from the postal authorities that we were bound by an international agreement under the International Postal Union. So the Council decided to test the agreement to see how far the totalitarians were living up to it. It composed a letter telling about what a fine country America was and how splendidly democracy was working in building up the defense arsenal, and so forth. This letter was mailed to considerable lists of persons under Hitler's, Mussolini's and Stalin's rule. The results have been what might be expected. As far as can be learned, these letters have not been received; in other words, the totalitarians have "broken" the international agreement. Their bluff has been called. In a way, of course, this was a stunt. It was designed to teach the American public rather than the Nazi public, but it points the way toward a much more comprehensive undertaking. It points toward a morale offensive for which we have not so far shaped any of the weapons, although it held a greater promise of keeping us out of war than any of the battleships and tanks which we have built with many times the amount needed.

America's 1917 Creel Committee

Do I advocate, then, another Creel Committee? A Ministry of Propaganda to rouse the spirit of America? I do not. No matter what our judgment, historically, on the work of that famous committee and its brilliant chairman might be (approximately forty out of fifty leading scholars in law, government, economics, and history, consulted on this subject recently, were inclined to question its methods), there can be no doubt that its work has been the inspiration of the propaganda methods of the totalitarian powers. Goebbels has publicly acknowledged his indebtedness. While it may be the right tool for his kind, it did not fit into our democratic pattern. Mr. Creel himself recognized the failure. He found himself helplessly standing by while the fundamental idea that the Committee on Public Information had tried to sell the world — a democratic peace — was crushed beyond recognition. Mr. Creel blames this failure upon Congress. But Congress is part of the pattern of our democracy and reflects but the sentiments of its constituents. Without cavil it must be admitted that the work of that committee has proved to be a boomerang as far as the defense of democracy is concerned.

What we do need and are slowly getting, as the Office of Government Reports under the able leadership of Mr. Lowell Mellett is expanding its work, is effective correlation and coordination of the information services of the several departments and agencies. Such a coordinated setup, unimaginable in 1917, is quite feasible today, since we have developed able staff workers in this field in practically all governmental offices. These men know each other well and constitute an effective working fraternity. Coordination of their efforts is today an urgent necessity. It has become abundantly clear that lack of integration in the official "news" of different government services causes cross eddies to develop in the public mind, resulting in confusion, even dismay. The public needs a clear sense of direction. Without it, the impression gets around that our defense effort is inept and inefficient. Such an impression will depress morale particularly among those people who are already inclined to look with admiration upon the totalitarian systems, their skill and effectiveness.

ENCOURAGING
DEMOCRACY IN EUROPE

THE MOST IMPORTANT and far-reaching task is still
to be done in yet another field. No private organization or
agency can possibly undertake it. What we must do is to sell
democracy abroad, particularly in Europe. We must spread
far and wide our own conviction that democracy is going to
win in the end. We must have people realize that we here
in America are aware of being engaged upon a gigantic enter-
prise, the biggest we have yet undertaken. We must speak
out decisively to this effect: that the world-wide reaction of
Fascism, of Hitlerism, of Stalinism, has made America dynamic,
has stirred the revolutionary embers of democratic faith in
the future, has roused America to do whatever is necessary to
destroy that reaction, root and branch. The creation of a special
unit to work with Latin America constitutes an important
beginning. But the task in Europe and Asia, although much
more difficult, is probably equally as important. Here the battle
of the mind broadens to world-wide dimensions. As in other
battles, so in this one, the best defense is attack. In fact, ideas
are the most potent weapons in the world, provided they are
challenging, virulent, and firmly believed in.

This means that we must bring forward the best minds
that can be had in America. Neither the mood of despondency
of the "lost generation" nor that smart-alecky contempt of
thought so characteristic of the ensuing era can help us in this
great crisis. Quite a few of the smartest boys have already
turned into hysterical crybabies. Their adulation of success
leaves them helpless in the face of the greatest success since
Napoleon — Adolf Hitler. Fortunately this country is rich

in real minds — poets and thinkers who can effectively bespeak the mind of America. It cannot be done in the self-satisfied manner of 1917-1918. Democracy is on trial, and its friends and believers will have to take a bold, self-critical stand today. The great depression has taught us a good deal; the rise of Hitler has taught us even more. There are deep underlying tensions in our society which we must face and fight. Anti-Semitism and other racial antagonisms, the plight of the unemployed and the general issue of the relations between labor and management—these and other "failures" of contemporary society have provided the psychic decomposition upon which the totalitarian movements have fed. There can be little doubt that the oversanguine expectations raised during the last war by the too effective work of American propaganda led to the violent despair in Europe afterwards. In a sense the cradle of Hitlerism is to be seen in those exaggerated hopes.

Broadcasting To Europe

What can we do? What morale offensive in Europe can we undertake in a practical way? I am not trying to give you a blueprint of the comprehensive campaign which needs to be plotted. I wish to mention but a few obvious things. I can already see the official in the Nazi Ministry of Propaganda blue-penciling this copy of the *Atlantic*, as he has done with all copies of the *Atlantic* since 1933. (Maybe, as he reads this, a little thought will creep into his mind as to whether the Nazis aren't going to be licked after all.) We should broadcast twenty-four hours, in French and German, on the most powerful beam to Europe. We are now doing it for two hours a day — to make it easy for the Gestapo to catch the listeners, I suppose. These broadcasts should mix much music and other entertainment (such as The Free Company's plays) with continuous news and informational spots. Over and over we should repeat the facts of our defense effort. The statistical curves of rising production and outlay should be told over and over again. Opinions should be kept at a minimum. The Nazis who listen in are put on their guard by our telling them that Hitler in our opinion is a bad man; the haters of Hitler throughout Europe need not be told.

Why French and German? Because with these two languages you can reach practically every person on the Continent who matters at this time. For instance, NBC has had continuous listener response from Switzerland to its German broadcasts. If we had been alert to our opportunities, we should have been in Turkey, Malta, and Egypt re-broadcasting on long wave our material to Italy, the Balkans, even France, during all these months. Maybe we could have rocked Italian morale to the breaking point before the present disasters bolstered it once again. Even now such opportunities do exist.

Printed Matter To Europe

We should continuously ship into Europe quantities of printed material, perhaps a weekly newspaper similar to that the Belgians got out during the World War, called *La Libre Belgique*. If only one-tenth of them reached their destination, they would spread new hope, a willingness to endure and to watch for opportunities to hamper the Nazi oppressors. We should also make certain that all American intermediaries who go to Europe for one purpose or another always think of themselves as emissaries of that new world which we in America are engaged in building.

But what is the use of all such efforts, many will ask. Can you hope to overthrow Hitler by such methods. You certainly can not. The situation is very different from 1918, owing to the despotic secret-police rule, the terror of the Nazis. But it is of the utmost importance for us, in the long run, to maintain the morale of our friends, of the believers in a democratic future. How important it is you can see from the continuous efforts Hitler is making to destroy that confidence. From the way he manhandled the German people, he knows how much depends upon making pulp of the hopes of those who do not accept his leadership. Obviously, what is good for him is bad for us. If we can maintain the morale of even limited sections of the people in France, in Belgium, in Czechoslovakia, in Greece, in Yugoslavia, in Holland, in Norway, in Poland, Spain, Austria, and even in Germany, we have gained just so many fighters for freedom at the decisive moment. Though these men and women are shackled right now, they will rise again. We must instill that confidence in them. We must continuously emphasize our interest in the extension of the democratic way of life. We are not fighting for Stalinism nor for imperialism. We are doing what we do, because of our faith in democracy's future.

Destruction Of Nazi Morale

But perhaps even more urgent is the destruction of the morale of the Nazis themselves. An impossible task? I don't think so. It is unrealistic to assume that their confidence is unshakable. There are many indications to the contrary. Many Nazi chiefs have maintained bank accounts in foreign countries; even American banks are reputed to have such accounts. Numerous Nazis are interned in concentration camps; others have been executed. The propaganda of the Goebbels ministry is designed to keep the mass cheered as much as it is to terrorize the opponents, or to "kid along" the luke-warm. A continuous morale offensive directed toward the Nazis and making them doubtful of the eventual outcome is going to be as decisive in the months and years ahead as the psychic support we give to the partisans of democracy in Europe. This argument holds as much or more for the would-be Nazis in the conquered nations, the Quislings, the Lavals, and the rest. Why are they for Hitler? Because they believe him to be "the future." There were such German, Dutch, Swedish, Polish partisans of Napoleon a hundred and thirty years ago. They thought they saw, with Hegel, the world spirit riding on a white horse, when they saw the little Corsican charging along after he had won another one of his battles. Yet, Napoleon "won all the battles." But did he win the war? He lost it, because he was on the side of despotism, on the side opposed to the future of freedom. The mind of Europe could not be won to such a cause. So, the more battles he won, the more enemies he found rising against him. Then, too, the great minds were rallied to the cause of freedom. The poets and the thinkers of England, Germany, and Italy, of nations large and small, and even those of France (at that time the first victim of despotic reaction) rose and won the battle of the mind.

Life has since become much more highly organized. The methods of mass communication require skilled and technically effective utilization. No country has a larger reservoir of master technicians in these fields than America. No country is more clearly predestined to undertake this offensive and to organize it. Not merely by the power of words, but more especially by the power of deeds successfully communicated to the masses of Europe, can this battle of the mind be won. These masses are today overwhelmed by a feeling of helplessness against fate. The infection has begun to spread to our own shores. We can take care of it here in a more or less routine way through the ordinary processes of our democracy. But to stop the plague and to ban it we must go to the cause of it. That is why we need a department for propagating the firm conviction that democracy is going to win. Our ideas and accomplishments will be its weapon. Without this armory America cannot be the arsenal of democracy that we are determined it shall be.

THE AUTHOR

CARL J. FRIEDRICH, Professor of Government at Harvard University, and at Radcliffe College, is the Chairman of the Executive Committee of the Council For Democracy.

Professor Friedrich is the author of several well known books including Constitutional Government and Politics and Foreign Policy in the Making. He is the director of the Harvard Radiobroadcasting Research Project, and conducts a seminar on Communications and Propaganda Analysis at the Graduate School of Public Administration.

In addition to this article from the Atlantic Monthly he is the author of "We Build The Future" which appeared in the January issue.

CPSIA information can be obtained
at www.ICGtesting.com
Printed in the USA
BVOW06s1635041017
496748BV00012B/70/P

9 781258 600051

Renal Diet Cookbook - Breakfast and Salads

52 Easy, Mouthwatering Breakfast and Salads Recipes that Include Sodium, Potassium and Phosphorous Amounts

Sabrina Sharp

Contents

Introduction

It is important to eat a wide variety of foods to stay healthy and strong. If you have kidney issues, then you are also advised to change your diet so as to consume smaller quantities of potassium, sodium, and phosphorous. This diet is referred to as the *renal diet*. Since everyone is different, patients with malfunctioning kidneys will have different dietary requirements to abide by. To get a meal plan that works for you, speak to a renal dietitian (a diet and nutrition consultant for people with kidney disease). A kidney-friendly diet will also help you protect your kidneys from further damage.

Breakfast Recipes

1. Easy Turkey Breakfast Burritos

Preparation time: 30 mins

Servings: 8

Ingredients

- 1 lb. ground turkey meat
- 8 burrito shells
- 2 tbsps. olive oil
- 8 eggs, beaten
- 1/4 cup sliced onions
- 1/4 cup fresh, chopped (green,
- yellow, or red) bell peppers
- 1 tbsp. jalapeño peppers, seeded
- 3 tbsps. fresh scallions, sliced
- 2 tbsps. fresh coriander, chopped
- 1/2 tsp. chili powder
- 1/2 tsp. smoked paprika
- 1 cup cheddar cheese, grated

Nutritional facts per serving

- Calories: 406cal
- Fat: 23g
- Sodium: 514mg
- Protein: 24g
- Potassium: 286mg
- Phosphorus: 360mg
- Carbohydrates: 22g

Steps

- Place the meatloaf, peppers, coriander, onions, and scallions in a pan with 1 tbsp. of olive oil and allow them to cook until the onion becomes transparent. Stir in

8

the spices, and then turn off the flame.

- Set another broad pan over a medium-high flame and add 1 tbsp. olive oil. When heated add the eggs and scramble until set.
- Place the desired quantities of the meatloaf blend, eggs, vegetables, and cheese in the burrito shells. Fold them and serve immediately.

2. Instant Omelet

Preparation time: 40 sec

Servings: 1

Ingredients

- 2 eggs
- 2 tbsps. water
- 1 tbsp. unsalted butter
- 1/2 cup seafood, meat, or vegetables

Nutritional facts per serving

- Calories: 256cal
- Fat: 14g
- Sodium: 144mg
- Protein: 12g
- Potassium: 123mg
- Phosphorus: 196mg
- Carbohydrates: 1g

Steps

- Beat the eggs and water together until they are properly blended.
- Heat butter in a 10-inch-long omelet pan or frying pan until it is hot.
- Pour the egg mixture into the pan.
- Check the sides and edges of the egg once it appears to solidify and then use a pancake turner to flip the egg.
- If desired, proceed to add cooked beef, seafood, or a half cup of vegetables to the omelet.
- Fold the omelet in half using the pancake turner. Then, slide the omelet off the pan and onto a plate to serve.

3. Blueberry Muffins

Preparation time: 30 mins

Servings: 12

Ingredients

- 1/2 cup unsalted butter
- 1 1/4 cups sugar
- 2 eggs
- 2 cups milk
- 2 cups all-purpose flour
- 2 tsps. baking powder
- 2 1/2 cups fresh blueberries
- 2 tsps. sugar (for the topping)

Nutritional facts per serving

- Calories: 276cal
- Fat: 10g
- Sodium: 210mg
- Protein: 5g
- Potassium: 122mg
- Phosphorus: 101mg
- Carbohydrates: 45g

Steps

- Mix the sugar and butter until they are smoothly blended together, utilizing a low-speed mixer.
- Add the eggs one at a time and keep whisking until they are combined.
- Combine the dry ingredients and mix them in with the other ingredients. Then, stir in some milk.
- Mash and stir in half a cup of blueberries. Then, add the remaining blueberries and mix them by hand.
- Spray the muffin cups with cooking spray and put them in the tin cups.
- Pour the muffin mixture into each muffin cup and sprinkle the muffin tops with honey.
- Bake for 25 to 30 minutes at 375°F. After confirming they are fully cooked, allow them to cool in a pan for at least 30 minutes.

4. Stuffed Breakfast Muffins

Preparation time: 25 mins

Servings: 12

Ingredients

- 2 cups flour
- 1 tbsp. sugar or honey
- 1/2 tsps. baking powder
- 1 tbsp. lime juice
- 8 tbsps. soft, unsalted butter
- 3/4 cup milk

Filling

- 4 eggs
- 8 oz. low-sodium bacon (1¼ sliced)
- 1 cup cheddar cheese, shredded
- 1/4 cup spring onions, sliced thinly

Nutritional facts per serving

- Calories: 331cal
- Fat: 24g
- Sodium: 329mg
- Protein: 11g
- Potassium: 153mg
- Phosphorus: 171mg
- Carbohydrates: 20g

Steps

- Preheat the oven to 425°F.

Prepare the filling

- Slightly under-cook the scrambled eggs.
- Fry the bacon until crispy.
- Add the remaining ingredients.

Prepare the dough

- Combine all the dry ingredients in a large container.
- Split with a pastry cutter or fork the unsalted butter till pea-size or small.
- In the middle of the blend, make a well, in the milk and lime juice and mix well.
- Start preparing the muffin tins by gently coating them with flour.
- Pour a little of the mix into each tin, then some filling, then again, some mix.
- Bake for 10/12 minutes or until they turn golden brown at 425°F.

5. Marshmallow Stuffing Chocolate Pancakes

Preparation time: 30 mins

Servings: 12

Ingredients

Filling

- 1 tbsp. unsweetened ground cocoa
- 1/4 cup heavy cream
- 1/2 cup melted cream cheese
- 1/2 cup marshmallow cream

Pancakes

- 1 cup flour
- 3 tbsps. sugar
- 3 tbsps. cocoa powder unsweetened
- 1/2 tsp. baking powder
- 1 tbsp. lime juice
- 1 egg
- 1 cup milk
- 2 tbsps. olive oil
- 2 tsps. vanilla extract
- 2/3 cup banana protein powder

Nutritional facts per serving

- Calories: 195cal
- Fat: 10g
- Sodium: 121mg
- Protein: 8g
- Potassium: 135mg
- Phosphorus: 135mg
- Carbohydrates: 23g

Steps

Marshmallow filling

- Beat the heavy cream and cocoa together until they form stiff peaks.
- Whisk it for another minute and then add the marshmallow cream, and cream cheese. Cover and put in the refrigerator.

Pancakes

- In a large container, combine all the dry ingredients together and set them aside.
- In a medium-sized bowl, combine all the wet ingredients together.
- Gently fold the dry ingredients into the wet ingredients, refraining from over-mixing.
- Prepare the pancakes at medium-high heat or 375°F on a finely oiled griddle.
- Make sure to flip the pancakes as they begin to bubble.
- Serve with the filling.

6. Homemade Buttermilk Pancakes

Preparation time: 10 mins

Servings: 9

Ingredients

- 2 cups all-purpose flour
- 1 tsp. cream of tartar
- 1 1/2 tsps. baking powder
- 2 tbsps. sugar
- 2 cups buttermilk
- 2 large eggs
- 1 tbsp. olive oil and 1/4 cup olive oil (divided)

Nutritional facts per serving

- Calories: 218cal
- Fat: 10g
- Sodium: 330mg
- Protein: 7g
- Potassium: 182mg
- Phosphorus: 100mg
- Carbohydrates: 28g

Steps

- In a wide bowl, mix the dry ingredients together and whisk 1/4 cup olive oil, eggs, and buttermilk.
- Heat a skillet over low heat.
- Add a tbsp. of oil to a pan. Scoop some of the pancake mixture into the skillet using a 1/3 measuring
- cup. Each pancake should be about 4 inches wide. Use a spatula to flip the pancakes once their edges
- start to brown and bubbles appear in the middle.
- Set the cooked pancakes aside.
- Serve with fresh berries or scrambled eggs.

7. Sirloin Cheddar Quiche

Preparation time: 40 mins

Servings: 6

Ingredients

- 1/2 lb. sirloin steak meat
- 1 cup onions, chopped
- 2 tbsps. canola oil
- 1/2 cup cheddar, shredded
- 5 eggs, beaten
- 1 cup cream
- 1 9" prepared piecrust
- 1/2 tsp. ground black pepper

Nutritional facts per serving

- Calories: 528cal
- Fat: 20g
- Sodium: 393mg
- Protein: 23g
- Potassium: 309mg
- Phosphorus: 282mg
- Carbohydrates: 23g

Steps

- Slice the trimmed sirloin into small pieces.
- Pour some oil in a pan and sauté the sliced steak and onions until the beef is browned. Put it aside for 10 minutes to allow it to cool slightly. Add the cheese to the pan.
- Beat the eggs and cream in a wide bowl and season with black pepper.
- Spread the steak and cheese mixture onto the piecrust rim. Then, pour over the top of the egg mixture and bake for 30 minutes at 350°F.
- Cover the foil with the cheesesteak quiche and switch the oven off. Enable the quiche to settle for 10 minutes before serving.

8. Spicy Tofu Scrambler

Preparation time: 25 mins

Servings: 2

Ingredients

- 1 tsp. olive oil
- 1/4 cup red bell pepper, diced
- 1/4 cup green bell pepper, chopped
- 1 cup solid tofu
- 1 tsp. onion powder
- 1/4 tsp. of garlic powder
- 1 garlic clove, chopped
- 1/8 tsp. turmeric

Nutritional facts per serving

- Calories: 214cal
- Fat: 14g
- Sodium: 25mg
- Protein: 19g
- Potassium: 468mg
- Phosphorus: 243mg
- Carbohydrates: 11g

Steps

- Pour some olive oil into a pan. Then, sauté the garlic and bell peppers in a medium sized, nonstick pan.
- Wash the tofu and place it in the pan while further breaking it with your wooden spoon. Add any remaining ingredients.
- Mix and cook until the tofu becomes a faint golden brown for around 20 minutes on medium heat. Wait until any excess moisture evaporates.
- Serve the tofu scrambler.

9. Baked Egg Cups

Preparation time: 25 mins

Servings: 2

Ingredients

- 3 cups cooked rice
- 4 oz. shredded cheddar cheese
- 4 oz. green chilies, diced
- 2 oz. drained and sliced pimentos
- 1/2 cup milk, skimmed
- 2 eggs, beaten
- 1/2 tsp. ground cumin
- 1/2 tsp. black pepper
- Nonstick cooking spray

Nutritional facts per serving

- Calories: 110cal
- Fat: 5g
- Sodium: 80mg
- Protein: 6g
- Potassium: 82mg
- Phosphorus: 92mg
- Carbohydrates: 14g

Steps

- Mix the rice, 2 ounces of cheese, chilies, pimentos, eggs, milk, pepper, and cumin in a wide dish.
- Apply nonstick cooking spray to the muffin cups.
- Split the mixture into the 12 muffin cups. Sprinkle the leftover shredded cheese on top of each cup.
- Bake for 15 minutes at 400°F until the muffins are fully done.

Preparation time: 30 mins

Servings: 1

Ingredients

- 2 large eggs
- 1/2 tsp. olive oil
- 1 pack of fresh basil
- 2 tbsps. grated Parmesan cheese
- 1/2 tsp. unsalted sunflower seeds
- 1/2 tsp. lime juice
- 1/2 tsp. lime zest
- 2 tbsps. diced red bell pepper
- 2 tbsps. sliced zucchini
- 2 tbsps. chopped Spanish onions
- 1/4 tsps. cayenne pepper
- 1/2 tsp. fresh chopped garlic

Nutritional fact per serving

- Calories: 309cal
- Fat: 23g
- Sodium: 296mg
- Protein: 21g
- Potassium: 410mg
- Phosphorus: 333mg
- Carbohydrates: 8g

Steps

- Apply cooking spray to the muffin tin.
- Crack an egg into each tin and add a few vegetables on top.
- Season with cayenne pepper.
- Bake for 10/15 minutes at 375°F.
- In the meantime, prepare the pesto in the food processor by pouring in the olive oil, basil, sunflower seeds, parmesan cheese, lemon zest, and lime juice. Pulse until a purée is formed.
- Place a dollop of pesto in the middle when the baked eggs come out of the oven.
- Serve and enjoy.

11. Strawberry Applesauce Pancakes

Preparation time: 20 mins

Servings: 4

Ingredients

- 2 cups all-purpose flour
- 1 tsp. cream of tartar
- 1 1/2 tsp. baking powder
- 2 cups rice milk
- 2 large eggs
- 2 tbsps. olive oil
- 2 cups halved strawberries
- 2 cups applesauce, without sugar

Nutritional facts per serving

- Calories: 394cal
- Fat: 6g
- Sodium: 590mg
- Protein: 11g
- Potassium: 451mg
- Phosphorus: 136mg
- Carbohydrates: 70g

Steps

- In a bowl, mix the dry ingredients together.
- In a separate bowl, combine the wet ingredients. Then, slowly combine and whisk together the contents of each bowl.
- Place the frying pan over medium-high heat and add some oil to it. Use a 1/3 measuring cup to scoop out pancake batter into the skillet. When bubbles emerge, flip the pancakes using a spatula. Allow them to brown on the other side.
- Serve with strawberries and applesauce.

12. Fruit & Cheese Omelet

Preparation time: 15 mins

Servings: 1

Ingredients

- 2 eggs
- 1 tsp. of water
- 1/4 cup of cottage cheese (low sodium)
- 1/2 canned, drained fruit salad
- Icing sugar (optional)

Nutritional facts per serving

- Calories: 217cal
- Fat: 11g
- Sodium: 129mg
- Protein: 20g
- Potassium: 259mg
- Phosphorus: 209mg
- Carbohydrates: 14g

Steps

- In a shallow cup, mix the eggs and water together.
- Spray a 8-inch nonstick skillet with cooking spray and allow it to heat up. Pour the egg mixture into
- it and allow the eggs to cook gently.
- Cook the omelet until the eggs are almost settled on the top but still look wet. Spoon the cottage cheese over them with 1/4 cup of fruit salad. Fold the omelet and place it on a tray.
- Place the omelet on a tray and serve with icing sugar (optional).

13. Breakfast Burrito

Preparation time: 15 mins

Servings: 2

Ingredients

- Nonstick cooking spray
- 4 eggs
- 3 tbsps. green, diced chilies
- 1/4 tsp. ground cumin
- 1/2 tsp. sweet pepper sauce
- 2 tortillas
- 2 tbsps. Salsa

Nutritional facts per serving

- Calories: 257cal
- Fat: 13g
- Sodium: 385mg
- Protein: 16g
- Potassium: 247mg
- Phosphorus: 185mg
- Carbohydrates: 21g

Steps

- Spray a medium-sized skillet with nonstick cooking oil and heat over a medium/high flame.
- Whisk the eggs in a bowl and mix with the green chili, cumin, and pepper sauce.
- Pour the eggs into the skillet and cook until the eggs become firm, stirring for one to two minutes.
- Heat the tortillas in an oven or a separate pan for 20 seconds.
- Divide the egg mixture between each tortilla and fold it like a burrito.
- Serve each with one tablespoon of salsa.

14. Applesauce Mint French Toast

Preparation time: 15 mins

Servings: 2

Ingredients

- 2 eggs, softly beaten
- 1/8 tsp. mint
- 1/2 cup milk
- 3/4 cup apple sauce
- 1 tsp margarine
- 4 bread slices

Nutritional facts per serving

- Calories: 353cal
- Fat: 9g
- Sodium: 463mg
- Protein: 13g
- Potassium: 255mg
- Phosphorus: 185mg
- Carbohydrates: 61g

Steps

- Mix the eggs, milk, and mint in a cup.
- Add applesauce to the mix.
- Over a medium-high flame, spread a dollop of margarine on a nonstick plate.
- Soak the slices of bread in the egg mixture and cook them over the skillet.
- Flip the bread and sear the other side until the bottom has browned.

15. Spinach & Cheese Omelet

Preparation time: 20 mins

Servings: 6

Ingredients

- 10 eggs
- 1 cup ricotta cheese
- 1 tbsp. freshly chopped herbs
- 1 tbsp. olive oil
- 1 medium-sized onion, chopped
- 2 cups of raw spinach

Nutritional facts per serving

- Calories: 221cal
- Fat: 16g
- Sodium: 175mg
- Protein: 17g
- Potassium: 256mg
- Phosphorus: 204mg
- Carbohydrates: 7g

Steps

- Preheat the oven to 350°F.
- In a nonstick, oven-proof plate, sauté the onion in olive oil.
- Add the spinach and sauté.
- Mix together the eggs, ricotta cheese, and fresh herbs in a separate bowl.
- Add the egg mixture to the dish.
- Finish cooking the omelet in the oven (around 10 minutes or until the top sets properly).
- Serve and enjoy.

Preparation time: 30 mins

Servings: 8

Ingredients

- 9"-long pre-made pastry shell
- 8 to 10 eggs
- 1/2 cup mushrooms, sliced
- 1/2 cup leeks, sliced
- 1 tbsp. olive oil
- 2 tbsp. grated parmesan cheese
- Black pepper
- Fresh thyme

Nutritional facts per serving

- Calories: 185cal
- Fat: 13g
- Sodium: 167mg
- Protein: 9g
- Potassium: 123mg
- Phosphorus: 102mg
- Carbohydrates: 12g

Steps

- Heat up the oven to 350°F.
- Sauté the cut leeks and mushrooms in one tablespoon of olive oil.
- Season with black pepper and thyme.
- Pour the sautéed leeks and mushrooms on the base of the pastry shell
- Then, whisk together the eggs and cheese and pour in the pastry shell over the leeks and mushrooms
- Bake until it sets, for approximately 30 minutes.

17. Lemon Apple Smoothie

Preparation time: 30 mins

Servings: 8

Ingredients

- 1/4 cup lime juice
- 1/2 cup apple juice
- 1 peeled and cored apple
- 1 banana
- 3 tsps. honey
- 1 cup frozen strawberry yogurt

Nutritional facts per serving

- Calories: 171cal
- Fat: 3g
- Sodium: 38mg
- Protein: 3g
- Potassium: 328mg
- Phosphorus: 60mg
- Carbohydrates: 39g

Steps

- Combine all the ingredients in a blender and pulse until they are creamy.
- Pour the smoothie mixture into the glasses.

18. Pumpkin Applesauce Bread or Muffins

Preparation time: 30 mins

Servings: 8

Ingredients

- 1/2 cup unsweetened applesauce
- 1 cup brown sugar
- 1/2 cup palm oil
- 2 eggs
- 2 cups all-purpose flour
- 1 tsp. baking soda
- 1/2 tsp. baking powder
- 2 tbsps. pumpkin pie seasoning

Nutritional facts per serving

- Calories: 253cal
- Fat: 1g
- Sodium: 142mg
- Protein: 4g
- Potassium: 83mg
- Phosphorus: 42mg
- Carbohydrates: 39g

Steps

- Preheat the oven to 425°F
- Spray oil across the muffin tins.
- Whisk the brown sugar, applesauce, eggs, and oil together in a medium-sized bowl.
- Mix the remaining items in a single medium-sized container.
- Add the applesauce mixture to the flour and whisk gently until just barely mixed.
- Pour the batter in a muffin pan or loaf.
- Bake for around 50 to 60 minutes if you are making a loaf or for around 20 minutes if you are making muffins.
- Poke a toothpick into a muffin and see if it comes out clean. If it does, proceed to take the muffins out of the oven and allow them to cool.

19. Quick Burritos

Preparation time: 10 mins

Servings: 2

Ingredients

- 1/2 tsp olive or canola oil
- 1/2 red bell pepper, thinly sliced
- 4 scallions, thinly sliced
- 8 eggs, beaten
- 4 (6"-long) maize tortillas

Nutritional facts per serving

- Calories: 230cal
- Fat: 14g
- Sodium: 138mg
- Protein: 15g
- Potassium: 212mg
- Phosphorus: 255mg
- Carbohydrates: 14g

Steps

- Heat the oil over low heat in a medium-sized frying pan.
- Add the scallions and bell pepper, sautéing them for around three minutes until tender.
- Add the eggs and mix them until the eggs are thoroughly cooked.
- Place the tortillas between two wet paper towels and put them on a dish.
- Heat the tortillas for two minutes in the oven.
- Spoon the mixture of eggs into the soft tortillas.
- Roll them up to eat.
- Try adding a drop of hot sauce or some chili powder to give it a slight kick.

Preparation time: 30 mins

Servings: 12

Ingredients

- 3 cups of master mix (check next recipe)
- 2/3 cup of water

Nutritional facts per serving

- Calories: 175cal
- Fat: 2g
- Sodium: 172mg
- Protein: 4g
- Potassium: 82mg
- Phosphorus: 52mg
- Carbohydrates: 19g

Steps

- Preheat the oven to 842°F
- Mix the ingredients together and allow the mixture to stand for five minutes
- Knead the dough about 15 times on a well-floured counter.
- Divide the dough into 12 pieces and shape into biscuits.
- Put the biscuits on a non-oil baking sheet.
- Bake until golden brown for 10 to 12 minutes.

Preparation time: 10 mins

Servings: 12

Ingredients

- 9 cups all-purpose flour
- 1tbsp. baking powder
- 2 tsps. cream of tartar
- 1 tsp. baking soda
- 1 1/2 cups powdered milk
- 2 1/4 cups vegetable shortening

Nutritional facts per serving

- Calories: 640cal
- Fat: 2g
- Sodium: 271mg
- Protein: 12g
- Potassium: 299mg
- Phosphorus: 190mg
- Carbohydrates: 68g

Steps

- Mix the flour, baking powder, cream of tartar, baking soda, powdered milk and shortening together.
- Store the contents in a cold, dry position in a big, airtight jar.
- Be sure to use it within 10 to 12 weeks.

22. Blueberry Pancakes

Preparation time: 20 mins

Servings: 3

Ingredients

- 1 1/2 cups sifted, all-purpose simple flour
- 2 tbsps. baking powder
- 3 tbsps. sugar
- 1 cup buttermilk
- 2 tsps. unsalted margarine
- 2 eggs, lightly beaten
- 1 cup blueberries

Nutritional facts per serving

- Calories: 224cal
- Fat: 7g
- Sodium: 197mg
- Protein: 8g
- Potassium: 129mg
- Phosphorus: 100mg
- Carbohydrates: 36g

Steps

- In a mixing cup, combine the baking powder, sugar, and flour.
- In the middle, create a well and add the remaining items gradually, steadily mixing throughout to create a thick batter.
- Heat a large 12-inch skillet or griddle and gently oil it.
- Proceed to cook the pancakes, tossing each once bubbles form around the edges.
- Serve immediately.

23. Vegan Breakfast Rice

Preparation time: 30 mins

Servings: 4

Ingredients

- 1 cup jasmine rice
- 2 tbsps. olive oil
- 1 cup cooked chickpeas
- 1 1/2 cups broccoli florets
- 2 tbsps. smoked paprika
- 1/2 tsp. cumin
- 1/4 tsp. powdered garlic
- 1/4 tsps. powdered onion
- 2 tbsps. chopped coriander
- 1/4 tsp. black pepper
- 1/4 cup of low-sodium vegetable stock
- 1/2 lime cut into 4 wedges

Nutritional facts per serving

- Calories: 347cal
- Fat: 13g
- Sodium: 291mg
- Protein: 9g
- Potassium: 455mg
- Phosphorus: 133mg
- Carbohydrates: 53g

Steps

- Cook the rice in accordance with the box's instructions.
- In a wide pan, heat the oil and stir fry the broccoli. Add the chickpeas, paprika, cumin, garlic powder, onion powder and pepper. Add the stock and cook until the broccoli is tender.
- Pour the rice into four individual platters. Cover the rice with the chickpeas and broccoli preparation, garnish with chopped coriander and a lime wedge and serve.

Preparation time: 30 mins

Servings: 4

Ingredients

- 1 cup milk
- 3 eggs
- 1/2 cup all-purpose flour
- 3 pieces bacon, chopped
- 1 cup spring onions, chopped
- 1 cup portobello mushrooms, chopped
- 1 cup green beans, chopped

Nutritional facts per serving

- Calories: 196cal
- Fat: 8g
- Sodium: 176mg
- Protein: 13g
- Potassium: 345mg
- Phosphorus: 195mg
- Carbohydrates: 23g

Steps

- Pre-heat the oven at 350°F.
- Whisk the eggs, flower and milk in a bowl, mixing thoroughly until smooth.
- Stir fry in a pan the bacon, onions, mushrooms for about 10 minutes; add the green beans and continue cooking until desired.
- Apply cooking spray to an 8×8" baking pan. Spread the cooked vegetables and bacon on the bottom of the pan and cover with the egg mix. Cook for about 30/35 minutes until the pie is set and golden brown.

25. Peach & Strawberry Smoothie

Preparation time: 5 mins

Servings: 3

Ingredients

- 1 cup frozen strawberries
- 1 peach, pitted and cubed
- 1/2 cup diced soft tofu
- 1 tbsp. agave syrup
- 1 cup rice milk

Nutritional facts per serving

- Calories: 130cal
- Fat: 4g
- Sodium: 54mg
- Protein: 7g
- Potassium: 262mg
- Phosphorus: 73mg
- Carbohydrates: 24g

Steps

- In a mixer, combine all the ingredients until creamy and serve.

26. Maple Seitan Sausage

Preparation time: 20 mins

Servings: 12

Ingredients

- 1 1/2 lb. ground seitan
- 1/2 tsp. black pepper
- 3/4 tsp. dry rosemary
- 1 pinch of nutmeg
- 1 tsp. smoked paprika
- 4 tbsps. parsley, chopped
- 2 tsps. maple syrup
- 1 tsp. water

Nutritional facts per serving

- Calories: 153cal
- Fat: 9g
- Sodium: 44mg
- Protein: 14g
- Potassium: 184mg
- Phosphorus: 130mg
- Carbohydrates: 2g

Steps

- In a large container, combine all the ingredients together.
- Refrigerate the seitan mix overnight or for at least four hours.
- Preheat the oven at 400°F
- Shape the mix into patties and bake in a skillet until it browns, around 15 minutes.

27. Spiced Paratha

Preparation time: 20 mins

Servings: 12

Ingredients

- 2 cups wheat flour
- 1 cup of water for kneading
- 1/2 tsp. cumin seeds
- 1/4 tsp. ground dry coriander
- 1/4 tsp. ground turmeric
- 1 tsp. oil

Nutritional facts per serving

- Calories: 133cal
- Fat: 3g
- Sodium: 1mg
- Protein: 1g
- Potassium: 129mg
- Phosphorus: 100mg
- Carbohydrates: 22g

Steps

- Knead in a bowl the flower, spices and water, until smooth; cover with cling film and let rest for
- around half an hour.
- Knead the dough and leave it to rest for 20 minutes.
- Divide the dough into 4 parts and shape like balls.
- Flatten the balls into paratha using a rolling pin and cook over a hot iron plate or pan.

Salads & Salad Dressings

1. Polynesian Rice Salad

Preparation time: 20 mins

Servings: 12

Ingredients

- 1 cup corn oil
- 1/2 cup vinegar (balsamic)
- 1 3/4 tsps. black pepper
- 3 garlic cloves
- 1/2 tsp. dried basil
- 1/2 tsp. dried oregano
- 1/2 cup fresh parsley
- 2 cups chopped tomatoes
- 1/2 cup red onion, sliced
- 1 cup frozen artichoke hearts
- 1/3 cup fresh dill
- 6 cups cooked white rice
- 1 lb. cooked prawns
- 1/2 cup dried cranberries
- 1 cup (canned) pineapple chunks
- 1 cup frozen green peas

Nutritional facts per serving

- Calories: 251cal
- Fat: 15g
- Sodium: 160mg
- Protein: 9g
- Potassium: 182mg
- Phosphorus: 77mg
- Carbohydrates: 24g

Steps

- Mix the pepper, salt, minced garlic, vinegar, minced parsley, oregano, basil, with the oil and vinegar. Set the mixture aside.
- Chop the onion and pepper.
- Boil the artichoke hearts and the green peas.
- Combine the tomatoes, onion, rice, artichoke hearts, shrimps, pineapple, dill, peas, and cranberries in a large container.
- Stir the dressing into the salad and serve.

2. No Salt Pesto

Preparation time: 20 mins

Servings: 12

Ingredients

- 4 tbsps. pine nuts
- 2 fresh garlic cloves
- 1 1/2 olive oil
- 1 bunch fresh basil leaves
- Juice of 1/2 a lime
- Black pepper

Nutritional facts per serving

- Calories: 95cal
- Fat: 10g
- Sodium: 65mg
- Protein: 1g
- Potassium: 40mg
- Phosphorus: 16mg
- Carbohydrates: 1g

Steps

- Put the olive oil, nuts, and garlic in a blender or food processor and pulse for a few seconds.
- Then, add the black pepper, basil leaves, and lime juice and proceed to blend until a dense, smooth paste is made. Add more lime juice and black pepper to taste.
- The mixture is then ready for usage. If you apply a thin coat of olive oil on top, it lasts for three to four days in the fridge. In ice cube trays, you can even freeze it and have convenient parts at any moment on standby.

3. Basil-Lime Pineapple Fruit Salad

Preparation time: 5 mins

Servings: 10

Ingredients

- 2 lbs. fresh pineapple chunks
- 1 lb. fresh strawberries
- 1 lb. fresh blueberries
- ½ cup granulated sugar
- 10g basil leaves
- Zest of 1 lime

Nutritional facts per serving

- Calories: 55cal
- Fat: 1g
- Sodium: 3mg
- Protein: 2g
- Potassium: 149mg
- Phosphorus: 19mg
- Carbohydrates: 13g

Steps

- Mix the pineapple with the sliced strawberries and blueberries.
- Place the sugar in a saucepan with ½ cup of water, turn on the heat and stir until dissolved.
- Turn off the heat, add the basil and lime zest and let cool.
- In a large bowl mix the pineapple, strawberries, and blueberries with the syrup. Chill before serving.

4. Chicken Apple Crunchy Salad

Preparation time: 5 mins

Servings: 4

Ingredients

- 4 chicken breasts, cooked
- (approximately 1 lb.)
- 1 large size gala apple
- 1/2 cup chopped celery
- 2 tbsps. chopped spring onions
- 2 tbsps. dried dark raisins or
- cranberries
- 4 tbsps. low-fat mayonnaise
- 1 tbsp. low-fat sour cream
- 1 tbsp. lime juice
- 1/4 tsp. cinnamon
- 1/4 tsp. black pepper

Nutritional facts per serving

- Calories: 245cal
- Fat: 13g
- Sodium: 222mg
- Protein: 22g
- Potassium: 351mg
- Phosphorus: 159mg
- Carbohydrates: 14g

Steps

- Dice the celery, apples, and onions.
- In a large bowl, mix the celery, chicken, raisins, apples, and spring onions together.
- Combine the black pepper, lime juice, whipped cream, mayonnaise, and cinnamon together.
- Add the dressing to the salad, toss thoroughly and serve.

5. Crunchy Couscous Salad

Preparation time: 5 mins

Servings: 4

Ingredients

- 1 medium-sized cucumber
- 1 red (sweet) pepper
- 1/2 sweet onion
- 2 tsps. black olives
- 2 tbsps. flat-leaf parsley, chopped
- 3 oz. uncooked couscous
- 1 cup of water
- 2 tbsp. olive oil
- 1 oz. vinegar
- 1 oz. feta cheese crumbled
- Black pepper
- Basil leaves

Nutritional facts per serving

- Calories: 130cal
- Fat: 7g
- Sodium: 168mg
- Protein: 4g
- Potassium: 110mg
- Phosphorus: 56mg
- Carbohydrates: 17g

Steps

- Slice the cucumbers thinly. Then, proceed to chop the onion, garlic, and peppers.
- Cook the couscous in boiling water, then drain and let cool
- Add the onion, cucumber, parsley, peppers, and olives to the couscous.
- To prepare the seasoning, mix together feta cheese, olive oil, salt, pepper, vinegar, and chopped basil.
- Mix the couscous salad and serve.

6. Curried Fruit & Chicken Salad

Preparation time: 5 mins

Servings: 4

Ingredients

- 4 boneless or skinless chicken
- breasts, cooked
- 1 celery stalk
- 1/2 cup chopped onions
- 1 medium-sized apple
- 1/2 cup seedless red grapes
- 1/2 cup seedless green grapes
- 1/2 cup water chestnuts
- 1 pinch of black pepper
- 1/2 tsp. curry powder
- 1 grated carrot
- 4 tbsps. Mayonnaise

Nutritional facts per serving

- Calories: 239cal
- Fat: 19g
- Sodium: 163mg
- Protein: 15g
- Potassium: 201mg
- Phosphorus: 116mg
- Carbohydrates: 7g

Steps

- Dice the chicken, apples, and celery. Proceed to drain and cut the water chestnuts.
- Combine the carrots, onions, celery, chicken, grapes, apple, water chestnuts, pepper, mayonnaise, and curry powder in a large salad bowl. Toss everything together. Instantly serve or chill for later use.

7. Tuna Pasta Salad

Preparation time: 10 mins

Servings: 4

Ingredients

- 2 cups cooked fusilli pasta
- 1 stalk of celery
- 1 red sweet pepper
- 2 ripe tomatoes
- 1 tbsp. spring onions
- 1 tbsp. lemon zest
- 2 oz. low-fat mayonnaise
- 2 oz. low-sodium Italian seasoning for salads
- 1 low-sodium, tuna can

Nutritional facts per serving

- Calories: 267cal
- Fat: 15g
- Sodium: 137mg
- Protein: 14g
- Potassium: 150mg
- Phosphorus: 104mg
- Carbohydrates: 22g

Steps

- Chop the celery, spring onions, tomatoes, and pepper. In a mixing bowl, combine the cooked pasta with the vegetables and the drained tuna.
- Whisk the salad dressing, lemon zest and mayonnaise together in a separate bowl and pour the dressing over the salad.
- To allow the flavors to mix thoroughly, refrigerate for one hour.

8. Italian Dressing

Preparation time: 5 mins

Servings: 16

Ingredients

- 1 tbsp. dried parsley
- 1/4 tsp. ground oregano
- 1/2 tsp. ground thyme
- 1/4 tsp. ground marjoram
- 1/2 tsp. ground celery seeds
- 1/4 tsp. garlic powder
- 1 tsp. granulated sugar
- 1 pinch black pepper
- 1/2 cup vinegar
- 1/2 cup olive oil

Nutritional facts per serving

- Calories: 66cal
- Fat: 9g
- Sodium: 19mg
- Protein: 1g
- Potassium: 11mg
- Phosphorus: 2mg
- Carbohydrates: 1g

Steps

- Mix the seasonings, vinegar, and oil together. Shake well to mix.

9. Flowers & Greens Salad

Preparation time: 5 mins

Servings: 4

Ingredients

- 4 spring onions
- 1 small-sized cucumber
- 1 cup snap peas
- 1 small-sized pear
- 3 oz. feta cheese
- 1 oz. edible flowers
- 2 tbsps. yogurt
- 2 tbsps. Pomegranate syrup
- 1 tbsp white vinegar
- 2 tbsps. chopped dill
- 4 tbsps. olive oil
- 1 tsp. mustard

Nutritional facts per serving

- Calories: 213cal
- Fat: 11g
- Sodium: 128mg
- Protein: 12g
- Potassium: 218mg
- Phosphorus: 164mg
- Carbohydrates: 12g

Steps

- Chop the spring onions and thinly slice the cucumber.
- Slice the snap peas, core and slice the pear. Mix all the vegetables in a bowl.
- Crumble the feta cheese with a fork.
- Mix the yogurt, lemon juice, syrup, olive oil, mustard, and dill together in a mixer.
- Toss the salad with the dressing.
- Scatter some festa cheese on the salad. Add the edible flowers on top and serve.

10. Thai Salad with Corn

Preparation time: 5 mins

Servings: 6

Ingredients

- Zest of 2 limes
- Juice of 1 lime
- 2 garlic cloves, minced
- 2 to tbsps. sweet chili sauce
- 1/2 cup sweet corn
- 1/2 red onion, finely chopped
- 1/2 cup coriander, minced
- 1/2 cabbage shredded
- 1/2 cup of carrots, shredded

Nutritional facts per serving

- Calories: 62cal
- Fat: 9g
- Sodium: 85mg
- Protein: 3g
- Potassium: 163mg
- Phosphorus: 15mg
- Carbohydrates: 15g

Steps

- In a small cup, mix the garlic, sweet chili sauce, lime juice, and zest together. Mix them together until everything is well blended and set it aside.
- Mix the remaining ingredients in a wide bowl and toss them until they are well combined.
- Serve immediately or within the next 24 hours.

11. Tabbouleh

Preparation time: 35 mins

Servings: 8

Ingredients

- 1 cup bulgur wheat
- 1 cup hot water
- 1 diced and tomato
- 1/2 medium-sized, seeded, and diced cucumber
- 1/2 cup chopped parsley
- 2 tbsps. green onion, thinly sliced
- 1 tbsp. chopped fresh mint
- 1 pinch of pepper
- 3 tbsps. olive oil
- 3 tbsps. lime juice

Nutritional facts per serving

- Calories: 115cal
- Fat: 6g
- Sodium: 8mg
- Protein: 4g
- Potassium: 181mg
- Phosphorus: 67mg
- Carbohydrates: 16g

Steps

- Pour the hot water into the bowl with the bulgur and let stand for 30 minutes.
- Mix the cucumber, tomato, parsley, mint, and green onion.
- Whisk the olive oil and lime juice with the pepper.
- Mix the cooked bulgur with the vegetables, add the dressing and mix well.
- Chill and serve.

12. Summer Salad

Preparation time: 5 mins

Servings: 4

Ingredients

- 1 lettuce head
- 8 strawberries, sliced
- 1 small red onion, chopped
- 1/4 cup slivered almonds, toasted
- 1 can mandarins, drained
- 1/4 cup olive oil
- 2 tbsps. (balsamic) vinegar
- 1 tsp. sugar
- 1 pinch of pepper

Nutritional facts per serving

- Calories: 251cal
- Fat: 3g
- Sodium: 96mg
- Protein: 6g
- Potassium: 266mg
- Phosphorus: 105mg
- Carbohydrates: 15g

Steps

- Combine the ingredients for the salad in a large salad dish.
- Place the sugar, olive oil, and balsamic vinegar in a jar and shake it to ensure everything is well blended.
- Add the dressing to the salad and toss.
- Serve and enjoy.

Preparation time: 5 mins

Servings: 4 to 6

Ingredients

- 1/2 cup raspberry vinegar
- 1/4 cup oil
- 1 tsp. french mustard
- 1 tbsp. sugar
- 1/4 cup mint leaves, sliced

Nutritional facts per serving

- Calories: 95cal
- Fat: 10g
- Sodium: 22mg
- Protein: 1g
- Potassium: 15mg
- Phosphorus: 3mg
- Carbohydrates: 4g

Steps

- In a small container, mix all the ingredients at once.
- Use as a salad dressing.

14. Pomegranate & Persimmon Salad

Preparation time: 5 mins

Servings: 12

Ingredients

- 6 cups of chopped lettuce
- 1/2 cup pomegranate seeds
- 1/2 cup cashews or pecans, sliced
- 2 tsps. basil leaves
- 1/4 cup raspberry vinegar
- 2 tbsps. olive oil
- 2 or 3 fresh persimmons
- 8 oz. crumbled feta cheese

Nutritional facts per serving

- Calories: 135cal
- Fat: 9g
- Sodium: 106mg
- Protein: 6g
- Potassium: 87mg
- Phosphorus: 69mg
- Carbohydrates: 10g

Steps

- Place the lettuce in a serving bowl.
- Mix the vinegar, basil, pomegranate seeds, oil, and almonds together.
- Add the dressing and mix thoroughly.
- Peel and chop the persimmons and place them on top of the lettuce, along with the crumbled feta cheese.
- Refrigerate and serve.

15. Pasta Salad with Roasted Red Pepper Sauce

Preparation time: 20 mins

Servings: 8

Ingredients

- 2 tbsps. mayonnaise
- 8 fresh basil leaves
- 1 garlic clove
- 2 tbsps. vinegar (balsamic)
- 2 canned roasted bell peppers
- 16 oz. penne pasta
- 1 tbsp. olive oil
- 1 large-sized yellow onion, diced

Nutritional facts per serving

- Calories: 266cal
- Fat: 6g
- Sodium: 86mg
- Protein: 9g
- Potassium: 151mg
- Phosphorus: 92mg
- Carbohydrates: 48g

Steps

- In a food processor or mixer, mix the garlic, vinegar, peppers, mayonnaise, and basil together.
- Cook the pasta according to the package's instructions. Then, drain it and rinse with cold water before setting it aside.
- Heat the oil over low heat in a medium-sized frying pan.
- Add the onion and sauté until it is caramelized and softened.
- In a large bowl, mix the penne, caramelized onions, and sauce together.
- Serve immediately or store in the refrigerator.

51

16. Exotic Mango Salad

Preparation time: 5 mins

Servings: 4

Ingredients

- 2 large-sized mangos, diced
- 2 red peppers, diced
- 3 tbsps. lemon juice
- 2 tsps. honey
- 4 tbsps. fresh, minced coriander
- 1 hot pepper, finely chopped

Nutritional facts per serving

- Calories: 152cal
- Fat: 2g
- Sodium: 6mg
- Protein: 2g
- Potassium: 407mg
- Phosphorus: 39mg
- Carbohydrates: 39g

Steps

- Toss all the ingredients together and cool for one hour in the freezer.
- Serve when ready.

17. Beet Salad

Preparation time: 50 mins

Servings: 4

Ingredients

- 4 beets cooked in the oven for 40 minutes
- 1/2 cup cashews
- 4 crunchy lettuce leaves
- 2 tbsps. cup fresh basil, finely chopped
- 1/2 cup balsamic vinegar
- 1tsps sugar
- 1tbsps water
- 2 tsps. olive oil
- 3 oz. crumbled blue cheese

Nutritional facts per serving

- Calories: 284cal
- Fat: 21g
- Sodium: 242mg
- Protein: 7g
- Potassium: 394mg
- Phosphorus: 103mg
- Carbohydrates: 17g

Steps

- Peel the cooked roots and cut them into cubes.
- In a saucepan, add the cashews, water, and sugar. Heat the liquid, stirring continuously until caramelized.
- Place the cashews mixture on a parchment paper foil, let cool and then chop as desired.
- Whisk the dressing in a bowl; mix vinegar, oil, and basil, then add the beets and mix thoroughly.
- Use the lettuce leaves as a bed for the salad.
- Scatter the caramelized chopped pecans and the crumbled cheese over the top and serve.

18. Buttermilk & Herbs Dressing

Preparation time: 5 mins

Servings: 2

Ingredients

- 1/2 cup mayonnaise
- 1/2 cup buttermilk
- 2 tbsps. vinegar
- 1 tbsp. fresh minced chives
- 1 tbsp. of dill
- 1 tbsp. dried oregano
- 1 pinch garlic powder

Nutritional facts per serving

- Calories: 84cal
- Fat: 4g
- Sodium: 65mg
- Protein: 2g
- Potassium: 10mg
- Phosphorus: 1mg
- Carbohydrates: 2g

Steps

- Whisk the mayonnaise, buttermilk, and vinegar together in a medium-sized bowl.
- Add the chives, a pinch of garlic powder, oregano, and dill. Mix thoroughly.
- To help the flavors mix well together, chill the dressing for at least one hour.
- Stir well with the dressing before using on salads, meat, fish, vegetables.

Preparation time: 50 mins

Servings: 10

Ingredients

- 1 cup mayonnaise
- 1 tbsp. horseradish
- 2 tsps. apple cider vinegar
- 3 tbsps. granulated sugar
- 2 tsps. fresh dill, finely chopped
- 1 lb. mixed coleslaw with carrots

Steps

- Whisk together the horseradish, mayonnaise, sugar, dill, and vinegar in a large bowl.
- Chill the salad for at least one hour or overnight (preferably) before serving.

Nutritional facts per serving

- Calories: 108cal
- Fat: 4.5g
- Sodium: 171mg
- Protein: 1g
- Potassium: 118mg
- Phosphorus: 12mg
- Carbohydrates: 9g

20. Peppers & Watermelon Salad

Preparation time: 50 mins

Servings: 6

Ingredients

- 3 cups seeded and diced watermelon
- 1 cup chopped green bell pepper
- 2 cups lemon juice
- 1 tbsp. coriander, minced
- 1 tbsp. spring onions, minced
- 2 medium jalapeños, chopped
- 1 garlic clove, minced

Nutritional facts per serving

- Calories: 31cal
- Fat: 0.4g
- Sodium: 3mg
- Protein: 2g
- Potassium: 129mg
- Phosphorus: 15mg
- Carbohydrates: 8g

Steps

- Mix all the ingredients together very well.
- Store the salad in the fridge for at least one hour.
- This salad is also perfect as a side for chicken or pork.

21. Crunchy Quinoa Salad

Preparation time: 15 mins

Servings: 8

Ingredients

- 1 cup rinsed quinoa
- 2 cups water
- 5 cherry tomatoes, chopped
- 1/2 cup cucumbers, chopped and seeded
- 3 green onions, chopped
- 4 tbsps. fresh mint, finely chopped
- 1/2 cup flat-leaf parsley, minced
- 2 tbsps. lemon juice
- 1 tbsp. grated lemon zest
- 4 tbsps. olive oil
- 4 tbsps. cup grated cheddar cheese
- 8 lettuce leaves

Nutritional facts per serving

- Calories: 159cal
- Fat: 10g
- Sodium: 47mg
- Protein: 6g
- Potassium: 238mg
- Phosphorus: 130mg
- Carbohydrates: 17g

Steps

- Rinse the quinoa until the water runs clear.
- Put the quinoa in a pan over medium heat with 1 tbsp. olive oil and sauté for two minutes, stirring continuously. Stir in two cups of water and bring it to a boil. Reduce the heat, cover the pan, and allow it to simmer for 10 minutes. Then, use a fork to fluff the quinoa.
- Combine the lime juice, mint, parsley, zest, and tomatoes with the olive oil, cucumbers, and onions. Add the cooled quinoa and mix again.
- Arrange the lettuce beds and divide the mixture between them. Scatter the cheese on top.

22. Lemon Orzo Spring Salad

Preparation time: 5 mins

Servings: 4

Ingredients

- 3/4 cup of orzo pasta
- 1/4 cup yellow pepper, cubed
- 1/4 cup red pepper, cubed
- 1/4 cup green pepper, cubed
- 1/2 cup of red spring onions,
- chopped
- 2 cups of zucchini, cubed
- 4 tbsps. olive oil
- 3 tbsps. fresh lime juice
- 1 tsp. lemon zest
- 3 tbsps. cheddar cheese, grated
- 2 tbsps. fresh rosemary, minced
- 1/2 tsp. black pepper
- 1/2 tsp. dried oregano
- 1/2 cup red pepper flakes

Nutritional facts per serving

- Calories: 331cal
- Fat: 23g
- Sodium: 80mg
- Protein: 7g
- Potassium: 377mg
- Phosphorus: 135mg
- Carbohydrates: 29g

Steps

- Cook the orzo pasta in accordance with the package directions and drain.
- In a wide pan over a medium-high flame, sauté the peppers, onions, and zucchini in two tbsps. of oil until they start to wilt.
- In a large bowl, whisk the lime juice, lime zest, 2 tbsps. of olive oil, cheese, rosemary, black pepper, red pepper flakes, and oregano. Add the orzo pasta, sautéed vegetables and mix thoroughly once again.
- Allow it to cool at room temperature or serve immediately.

23. Cold Shrimps Noodle Salad

Preparation time: 5 mins

Servings: 10

Ingredients

- 1 lb. cooked and cooled pasta
- 4 cups of cooked shrimp
- 1 cup chopped scallions
- 2 cups cooked broccoli florets
- 1 cup chopped carrots
- 2 cups fresh, chopped shitake
- mushrooms
- 2 tbsps. sesame oil
- 2 tsps. chili oil
- 1/2 cup white rice vinegar
- 2 tbsps. chopped garlic
- 1 tbsp. fresh, chopped ginger
- 1/4 cup low-sodium soy sauce
- 1/4 cup fresh lemon juice
- 1 tbsp. lemon zest

Nutritional fact per serving

- Calories: 255cal
- Fat: 12g
- Sodium: 434mg
- Protein: 14g
- Potassium: 326mg
- Phosphorus: 230mg
- Carbohydrates: 28g

Steps

- Combine the pasta, shrimps, scallions, broccoli, mushrooms and carrots in a large salad bowl.
- Use a mixer to blend together the rest of the ingredients for around one minute.
- Add the pasta and vegetables mixture to the dressing mix, toss until it is well coated, and then serve immediately.

24. Pea Salad with Ginger-Lime Dressing

Preparation time: 10 mins

Servings: 6

Ingredients

- 1 cup sugar snap peas
- 1 cup snow peas
- 1 cup thawed, fresh sweet peas

Dressing

- 1 tsp. low-sodium soy sauce
- 1/4 cup fresh lemon juice
- 1 tsp. fresh lemon zest
- 2 tsps. fresh ginger fresh, chopped
- 1/2 cup olive oil
- 1 tbsp. hot sesame oil
- 1 tbsp. sesame seeds
- 1 pinch black pepper

Nutritional facts per serving

- Calories: 226cal
- Fat: 7g
- Sodium: 71mg
- Protein: 4g
- Potassium: 118mg
- Phosphorus: 41mg
- Carbohydrates: 7g

Steps

- In a hot skillet, gently toast the sesame seeds, flipping them continuously for around three to five minutes.
- Blanch all three types of peas for two minutes in a big pot of boiling water over high heat. Drain and then place in an iced water bowl. Stain when cooled.
- Mix the lemon juice and zest, black pepper, and soy sauce in a small bowl for around two minutes
- Continue whisking and add the ginger, olive oil and sesame oil.
- Combine the salad dressing with the pea mix in a large serving dish. Scatter the toasted sesame seeds on top and serve.

25. Shrimps & Couscous Salad

Preparation time: 15 mins

Servings: 4

Ingredients

- 1 1/2 cups of water
- 1 cup couscous, uncooked
- 1 lb. cooked shrimp
- 1 1/2 cups red pepper, chopped
- 1/4 cup green onions, diced
- 1/2 cup fresh basil, chopped
- 1/4 cup low-sodium chicken broth
- 3 tbsps. fresh lime juice
- 1 tbsp. olive oil

Nutritional facts per serving

- Calories: 341cal
- Fat: 9g
- Sodium: 811mg
- Protein: 27g
- Potassium: 376mg
- Phosphorus: 445mg
- Carbohydrates: 41g

Steps

- Cook the couscous in boiling water according to the package directions.
- Fluff with a fork and allow it to cool.
- In a large container, mix the seafood, couscous, basil, green onions, and peppers together.
- For the dressing, whisk in a small bowl the broth, lemon juice, and olive oil. Pour the dressing over the salad, toss gently and serve.

CPSIA information can be obtained
at www.ICGtesting.com
Printed in the USA
BVHW091103230621
610212BV00010B/1660